A SELECTIVE GUIDE TO THE MICROCOMPUTER LITERATURE

Allan D. Pratt

Graham Conley Press
Tucson, Arizona

Graham Conley Press

Production supervision provided by

WORD SMITH

Wordsmith Graphic Communications

TABLE OF CONTENTS

NOTE TO READERS

Any work of this type suffers from two drawbacks. First, the selection of items included is inevitably to some degree subjective, and even the most diligent compiler is liable to errors and omissions. Second, there is a continual flow of new items being published, so this work will rapidly become dated.

If you find that your favorites have been omitted, or that some item included is in your opinion unsuitable, please write the author with your suggestions at the address below. Similarly, please write if some new item comes to your attention which you feel should be included. All suggestions and recommendations will be carefully considered for a subsequent edition of this work.

Graham Conley Press
2509 N. Campbell Ave, #284
Tucson AZ, 85719

INTRODUCTION

Within the last few years there has been a sudden upsurge in interest in small computers, variously called "home computers", "personal computers" or "microcomputers". These small computers are typically priced in the $400 to $2000 range and are usually purchased by individuals for their own use at home or at work. The widely advertised Apple, TRS-80 and VIC-20 are typical examples. There is now even a $100 microcomputer on the market, the Sinclair ZX-81, which is also being sold as the Timex 1000.

This upsurge has been paralleled by a similar growth in publications relating to the field. New journals appear almost weekly; new books are announced with equal frequency. Many bookstores now have extensive sections devoted solely to this topic. Naturally, there has also been a greatly increased demand for these materials in library collections. This guide has been prepared to assist librarians in making selections in this new and often confusing area.

This guide is organized into several sections. The first deals with the periodical literature, the second with books. These are followed by a short section on reference works and publications relating to the use of microcomputers in the library. The last consists of alphabetical listings of the periodicals and books by title and a directory of publishers' addresses.

PERIODICALS

In all, there are now over 300 different periodicals of highly varying frequency and quality. This guide is not an exhaustive listing. Only some thirty-odd of the more common periodicals are included. The journals can be divided into a number of categories based on the audiences for which they are intended. First there is the "General" category. These journals are intended for any user of a microcomputer, regardless of which system is owned. These general magazines can be further subdivided into "Introductory" and "Advanced" categories. Popular Computing and Personal Computing are instances of the first category, while BYTE and Microcomputing are instances of the second.

The second group is "System Specific". That is, these journals are intended for those who have a specific microcomputer; e.g. Softalk is for Apple owners, 80-Microcomputing is for TRS-80 owners. This category also includes those journals which focus on a particular micro-related theme, such as a specific operating system, or a specific central processor unit (CPU). It also includes the only example thus far of a periodical devoted to a specific program.

Two types of publications have been specifically excluded from this guide. The first of these are the "Applications" periodicals. There are many small publications, mostly newsletters, which deal with micros in a specific profession; e.g. "Micros in Dentistry", "Agricultural Microcomputing", etc. (These are imaginary, simply illustrative, examples). These are virtually impossible to track down in any comprehensive way. To locate such items, it is probably best to contact the professional society in the area of interest. The other excluded titles are the "user group" publications. There are many computer clubs of different kinds all over the country, many of which publish newsletters. However, only periodicals which are more or less "commercial" are covered here.

GENERAL

INTRODUCTORY LEVEL

Creative Computing. PO Box 789-M, Morristown, NJ 07960. Monthly. $15/yr. (ISSN 0097-8140)
Probably the least technical. Light style. Runs many game programs (guessing games, tic-tac-toe, etc). Cartoons, occasional fiction. Probably the best choice for school libraries.

Desktop Computing. PO Box 917, Farmingdale, NY 11737. Monthly. $27/yr. (ISSN 0731-3616)
Small business oriented. Advertised as being written without computer jargon.

Interface Age. 16704 Marquardt Ave., Cerritos, CA 90701. Monthly. $18/yr. (ISSN 0147-2992)
Subtitled "Computing for Home and Business Applications." Mostly software and systems evaluation articles. Aimed at the business or professional user.

Personal Computing. 50 Essex St., Rochelle Park, NJ 07662. Monthly. $14/yr. (ISSN 0192-5490)
"For Your Home and Business". For the serious or semi-serious user. Not for game-playing.

Popular Computing. PO Box 307, Martinsville, NJ 08836. Monthly. $15/yr. (ISSN 0194-8075)
Successor to the quarterly OnComputing. Primarily aimed at the home user.

ADVANCED LEVEL

BYTE. 70 Main St., Peterborough, NH 03458. Monthly. $15/yr. (ISSN 0360-5280).
One of the major journals in the field. Carries a mix of hardware, software, and system design articles.

Dr. Dobbs' Journal. PO Box E., Menlo Park, CA 94025. 10 issues per year. $15/yr. (ISSN 0190-1435)
Highly technical. Much assembly language programming, articles on esoteric languages and hardware.

Infoworld. 530 Lytton Ave., Palo Alto, CA 94301. Weekly. $18/yr. (ISSN 0199-6649).
Newspaper format. Trade paper of the microcomputer industry. Covers news, rumors, business and technical aspects of the field.

Microcomputing. PO Box 997, Farmingdale, NY 11737. Monthly. $25/yr. (ISSN 0192-4575)
Another major journal. Formerly titled Kilobaud Microcomputing. Carries hardware, software, design and applications articles.

SYSTEM SPECIFIC

APPLE

The Apple Orchard. 910A George St., Santa Clara, CA 95050. Bimonthly. $15/yr. (ISSN 0277-1950)

Nibble. PO Box 325, Lincoln, MA 01773. 8 issues per year. $17.50.

Softside. 100 Pine St., Holmes, PA 19043. Monthly. $30/yr. (ISSN 0274-8630)

Softalk. 11021 Magnolia Blvd., North Hollywood, CA 91601. Monthly. Special school and library rate, $8/yr. (ISSN 0274-9629)

ATARI

A.N.A.L.O.G. 400/800 Magazine. P.O. Box 615, Holmes, PA 19043. Bimonthly. $12/yr. Articles, tutorials, software reviews, program listings in BASIC and Assember for the Atari 400 and 800.

Antic: The Atari Resource. 297 Missouri St., San Francisco, CA 94107. Bimonthly. $15/yr.
Software reviews, programs, articles.

COMMODORE

Commodore Magazine. 681 Moore Rd., King of Prussia, PA 19406. Bimonthly. $15/yr.
Official publication of Commodore Inc. Articles, product news, etc. about PET/CBM.

Power/Play. 487 Devon Park Rd., Wayne, PA 19087. Quarterly. $10/yr.
For home users of Commodores. New product news, applications, games, programming tips.

CP/M BASED SYSTEMS

Lifelines. 1651 Third Ave., New York, NY 10028. Monthly. $18/yr. (ISSN 0279-2575).
From the CP/M users' group. Editorials, reviews, new programs, bug fixes, new products.

Microsystems. 39 E. Hanover Ave., Morris Plains, NJ 07950. Bimonthly. $10/yr. (ISSN 0199-7955)
Covers equipment using the S-100 bus and the CP/M operating system. Formerly S-100 Microsystems.

IBM PERSONAL COMPUTER

Softalk for the IBM Personal Computer. 11021 Magnolia Blvd., North Hollywood, CA 91601. Monthly. $24/yr.

PC: The Independent Guide to IBM Personal Computers. 1528 Irving St., San Francisco, CA 94122. Monthly. $27/yr.

Personal Computer Age. PO Box 70725, Pasadena, CA 91107. Monthly. $18/yr.

OSBORNE I

The Portable Companion. 26500 Corporate Ave., Hayward, CA, 94545. Bimonthly. (ISSN 9732-7501)

PET/CBM -- See COMMODORE

TEXAS INSTRUMENTS

99'er Magazine. PO Box 5537, Eugene, OR 97405. Bimonthly. $18/yr.
Covers TI 99/4A and other 16-bit Texas Instruments computers.

TRS-80

80-Microcomputing. PO Box 981, Farmingdale, NY 11137. Monthly. $15/yr. (ISSN 0199-6789)
Largest, most widely read journal on all models of the TRS-80.

80-US: The TRS-80 Users' Journal. 3838 S. Warner St., Tacoma, WA 98409. Bimonthly. $18/yr.

VISICALC

SATN: The Journal for Visicalc Users. 27 Mica Lane, Wellesley, MA 02181. Bimonthly. $30/yr.
Covers extensions, elaborations, and advanced use of the Visicalc spreadsheet program.

ZX-81, (TIMEX 1000)

SQ, The Syntax Quarterly. Bolton Rd. R.D. 2, Box 457, Harvard, MA 04151. Quarterly. $15/yr. (ISSN 0734-0133)

SYNC. 39 E. Hanover Ave., Morris Plains, NJ 07950. Bimonthly. $10/yr.

SYNTAX. Bolton Rd. R.D. 2, Harvard, MA 04151. Monthly. $29/yr. (ISSN 0273-2696) Newsletter.

BOOKS

The outpouring of books in this area is remarkable. There are by now several hundred titles. Most of the major publishers such as McGraw-Hill have several titles in print. However, many of the microcomputer monographs come from small, specialized publishers, such as Tab Books, Dilithium Press and Sybex. The titles are almost always published in paperback. The field is so volatile that publishing in hardcover is rare especially by the smaller firms. Many of these titles are published by very small, specialized companies which are not "publishers" in the traditional sense. To further confuse matters, their books are sometimes distributed by major publishers, often with little indication that this is the case.

One particular instance will illustrate this difficulty. Management Information Source of Portland Oregon, has thus far published three titles. The first two of these were The Power of: Visicalc (vols 1 and 2). They have no ISBNs. The third one The Power of: Supercalc is identical in format and publisher's data except for two minor points. On the front cover is a symbol for "Spectrum Books", and an adhesive label has been pasted on the back cover with an ISBN which identifies it as a Prentice-Hall book. "Spectrum" is a Prentice-Hall series. However, there is no other indication anywhere that P-H has any connection with the book.

These titles can be grouped into categories along the same lines as the periodicals, except that there are many more different kinds of books. The broadest category is the "Computer Literacy" group. Here some works not specifically dealing with micros have been included because of their broad interest. These are non-technical examinations of the microprocessor field or historical accounts of computers in general.

Next, there is a "System Selection" category. These titles are written for the businessperson considering acquiring a system for office or factory use. These emphasize the economic pros and cons of various options. A few are aimed at the individual considering a micro for home use. Both are aimed at the reader before a purchase decision is made.

The next category, "Introductory Programming" includes titles which teach the BASIC programming language. Many of these are aimed at children who have access to a micro and want to be able to do something with it. Young children are among the most avid microcomputer users, so many of these are written in a simple and entertaining manner.

Adults could learn the elements of programming from these works if they were not offended by the style. However, there are a number of "Introductory Programming" works written for adults. The main difference between the adult and juvenile works lies in the examples and programs. The children's works focus on games and colorful graphic displays while the adult works use practical examples such as check-book balancing. Nearly all the introductory programming titles are aimed at some specific microcomputer. Thus, this category has been subdivided into sections for the various types of micros.

Once past the introductory stage, the field fragments in several directions. Microcomputer users fall into two very broad general categories: those who want to write their own programs for their own purposes and those who prefer to use programs written by others. The former group typically is the home/hobby user while the latter is usually the business user.

Most of the books in the field are for the former group -- those who want to write their own programs. The most popular theme within this group of books for programmers is "BASIC Applications". These give programs and examples in the BASIC language for particular kinds of uses, such as accounting, engineering, mathematics, etc. Another group is "Advanced BASIC" in which the focus is on explaining methods, techniques and special features which are not explained in the ordinary manuals.

The next largest category in the programming group is the "Other Languages" category. While BASIC is easily the most widely used programming language for micros, there are a number of others such as Pascal, FORTH, PL/M, LOGO, and C. Many of these are specific to a particular brand of micro or a particular version of a language.

The most technical and detailed of the programming books is the "Assembly Language" group. These treat programming at the most detailed and complex level and are strictly for the specialists. These, perforce, are very specific to a particular microprocessor.

There is also a "Systems Design" group. These books are not necessarily devoted to a single programming language, though some are. They aim to teach the reader how to design a program or how to find errors in one, rather than teach the mechanics of a particular language.

For those who are primarily interested in using programs already written and available, there are two general categories. The first of these is "Operations and Maintenance." These cover procedures and good operating practices so that the micro will continue to perform as it should. They assume you have a micro on hand, and need to know more about how to take care of it, or use some of its special features.

The other category is "Program Support". There are several commercially available programs which have a great deal of flexibility -- more than most users would consider, and more than is explained in the manuals which were supplied with the program. Also, it is unfortunately true that sometimes the manuals supplied with these programs are badly written, erroneous or unclear. Thus, books devoted to the explication and elaboration of these programs are beginning to appear. Not many books of this type have yet been published, but more will surely appear soon.

In summary, the ad-hoc classification of books in this area is:

I. Computer Literacy

II. System Selection

III. For Programmers

A. Introductory Programming
B. BASIC Applications
C. Advanced BASIC
D. Other Languages
E. Assembly Language
(A-E subdivided by type of micro)
F. Systems Design

IV. For Users

A. Operations and Maintenance
B. Program Support

COMPUTER LITERACY

The Analytical Engine: Computers -- Past, Present and Future. Jeremy Bernstein. Morrow, NY. 1981. 128p. $4.95. (ISBN 0-688-00488-1)
Good brief history of computers.

Computer Choices. H. Dominic Covvey and Neil Harding McAlister. Addison-Wesley, Reading, MA. 1982. 225p. $8.95. (ISBN 0-201-10113-0)
Deals with both practical and technical issues. They imply that computers have been oversold and given a false sense of importance. Somewhat of a "debunking" title.

Computer Consciousness: Surviving the Automated 80's. H. Dominic Covvey and Neil Harding McAlister. Addison-Wesley, Reading, MA. 1980. 211p. $8.95. (ISBN 0-201-01939-6)
Pulls together a wide range of "buzz words" and describes them in context. Explains much of the current technical terminology.

Computer Power and Human Reason: From Judgment to Calculation. Joseph Weizenbaum. W. H. Freeman, San Francisco. 1976. 300p. $10.95. (ISBN 0-7167-0463)
Excellent philosophical and scientific critique of computers, their uses and abuses. Highly recommended.

Computers in Your Life. Melvin Berger. Crowell, NY. 1981. 128p. $9.57. (ISBN 0-609-04100-4)
Aimed at the junior high student. The author is a well-known writer for young adults.

The Electronic Cottage. Joseph Deken. Bantam Books, NY. 1981. 386p. $3.95. (ISBN 0-553-22863-3)
Popular exposition of the potential uses of micros in the home especially for "telecommuting" to work.

Exploring with Computers. Gary Bitter. Messner, NY. 1981. 64p. $7.95. (ISBN 0-671-34034-4)
Written for fifth, sixth and seventh grade pupils. Straightforward and unpatronizing.

How You Can Learn to Live with Computers. Harry Kleinberg. Penguin, London. 1978. $2.95. (ISBN 0-14-004970-3)
Despite the unfortunate choice of title, this is an excellent non-technical view of what goes on inside computers, what they can and cannot do and of their potential impact.

The Micro Millenium. Christopher Evans. Washington Square Press, NY. 1981. 308p. $3.50. (ISBN 0-671-42184-0)
By a late well-known computer scientist and psychologist. Suggests that microtechnology will have a very strong impact on current society.

The Microelectronics Revolution: The Complete Guide to the New Technology and Its Impact on Society. Tom Forrester. (ed.) MIT Press, Cambridge, MA. 1980. 589p. $12.50. (ISBN 0-262-56021-6)
Anthology of articles from the popular and business press over the last five years. Discusses the impact of microelectronics from several points of view.

The Personal Computer Book. Peter A. McWilliams. Prelude Press, Los Angeles. 1982. $11.95. (ISBN 0-931580-90-0).
Best non-technical, non-jargon book for the layman yet published. Clear, accurate, and humorous. Highly recommended.

Robots on Your Doorstep: A Book about Thinking Machines. Nels Winkless and Iben Browning. Robotics Press, Beaverton, OR. 1978. 179p. $9.95. (ISBN 0-89661-000-4)
Curious and thought-provoking book on the theme. Observations on human and artificial intelligence and on the likely developments of the latter in the near future.

The Soul of a New Machine. Tracy Kidder. Avon, NY. 1980. 293p. $3.95 (ISBN 0-380-59931-7)
Well-written and accurate narrative of the engineers and scientists involved in the design of a new computer. Pulitzer Prize winner in 1982.

Without Me You're Nothing: The Essential Guide to Home Computers. Frank Herbert with Max Barnard. Simon & Schuster, NY. 1981. 304p. (ISBN 0-671-43964-2)
By a noted science fiction writer. One of the best and most imaginative introductions to the subject.

The Word Processing Book. Peter A. McWilliams. Prelude Press, Los Angeles. 1982. $11.95.
Similar to The Personal Computer Book above. Clear, concise, well written. Highly recommended. The two books by McWilliams are clearly the best choices as introductory adult works on this subject.

SYSTEM SELECTION

Basic Business Software. E. G. Brooner. Sams, Indianapolis, IN. 1981. 140p. $9.95.
A successful attempt to demystify small computers. Focuses on how one can evaluate the wide variety of what is available. The "Basic" in the title refers to "fundamental" or "essential", not the programming language of the same name.

Business System Buyer's Guide. Adam Osborne and Steve Cook. Osborne/McGraw-Hill, Berkeley, CA. 1981. 165p. $7.95. (ISBN 0-931988-47-0)
By one of the most respected writers in the field. Excellent manager's guide. Written before Osborne formed his own computer manufacturing company and thus not biased toward his own system.

Computers for Everybody. (2d ed.) Jerry Willis and Merle Miller. Dilithium Press, Beaverton, OR. 1982. 272p. $7.95. (ISBN 0-88056-094-0)
The first edition was chosen by Library Journal as one of the 100 outstanding Sci-Tech books of 1981.

Home Computers: A Simple and Informative Guide. Scott Corbett. Little, Brown, NY. 1980. 118p. $4.95. (ISBN 0-316-15658-2)
For home, rather than business users. Also suitable for high school age readers.

How to Buy the Right Small Business Computer System. C. Roger Smolin. Wiley, NY. 1981. 156p. $8.95. (ISBN 0-471-08494-8)
Covers evaluation, pricing and installing of a small business system and the necessary changes in the business which will result.

How to Computerize Your Small Business. Jules A. Cohen. Prentice-Hall, NY. 1980. 171p. $7.95.
Selection and installation criteria for the small businessman considering a micro.

Personal Computing: Home, Professional and Small Business Applications. (2d ed.) Daniel R. McGlynn. Wiley, NY. 1981. 355p. $14.95. (ISBN 0-471-86164-2)
Comprehensive survey of features and limitations of commercially available hardware and software. Describes several programming languages. Lists software suppliers, equipment manufacturers.

Small Computers for the Small Businessman. Nicholas and Sharon Rosa. Dilithium Press, Beaverton, OR. 1980. 340p. $16.95. (ISBN 0-918398-31-2)
Excellent, clear expositions of the theme. The advice is pragmatic and practical. Particularly valuable in introducing concepts one needs before visiting the computer store. Also points out things which can be ignored with no penalty.

Word Processors and Information Processing: A Basic Manual on What They Are and How to Buy. Dan Poynter. Para Publishing, Santa Barbara, CA. 1982. 170p. $11.95. (ISBN 0-9155-16-31-4)
A non-technical guide by a professional writer who has used WP systems to produce five books.

Your First Computer: A Guide to Business and Personal Computing. Rodnay Zaks. Sybex, Berkeley, CA. 1980. 258p. $7.95.
Presents criteria to simplify selection among the wide range of possible options for either home or business use.

FOR PROGRAMMERS

INTRODUCTORY PROGRAMMING

GENERAL TEXTS

Basic: An Introduction to Computer Programming Using the BASIC Language. (3d ed.) William F. Sharpe and Nancy L. Jacob. Free Press, Glencoe, IL. 1979. $7.95. (ISBN 0-02-928390-6)

Basic Programming. (3d ed.) John G. Kemney and Thomas E. Kurtz. Wiley, NY. 1980. 334 pp. $13.95. (ISBN 0-471-01863-5) Kemney and Kurtz are the creators of BASIC, though it has grown far beyond their original intentions.

Bit of BASIC. Thomas Dwyer and Margot Critchfield. Addison-Wesley, Reading, MA. 1980. 192p. $5.95. (ISBN 0-201-932538-04-5)

Computer Programming for the Complete Idiot. Donald McCann. Design Enterprises of San Francisco, San Francisco. 1979. 126p. $6.95. (ISBN 0-932538-04-5)

Elementary BASIC. Henry Ledgard and Andrew Singer. Random House, NY. 1982. 264p. $12.95. (ISBN 0-394-70789-3) Pastiches of Sherlock Holmes stories used to illustrate and teach the elements of BASIC.

Instant Freeze-Dried Computer Programming in BASIC. (2d ed.) Jerald R. Brown. Dilithium Press, Beaverton, OR. 1982. 195p. $12.95. (ISBN 0-918398-57-8)
For any microcomputer using a version of Microsoft BASIC.

An Introduction to Microcomputers: Volume 0, The Beginners Book. (3d ed.) Adam Osborne and David Bunnell. Osborne/McGraw-Hill, Berkeley, CA. 1982. 233p. $12.50. (ISBN 0-931988-64-0)
First of a 4 volume set. Deals with hardware and circuits. Well regarded in the field.

Introduction to Microcomputers: Volume 1, Basic Concepts. (2d ed.) Adam Osborne. Osborne/McGraw-Hill, Berkeley, CA. 1980. $12.99. (ISBN 0-931988-34-9)
Second of the series. Detailed coverage of the principles of operation.

APPLE

APPLE Basic. Richard Haskell. Prentice-Hall, Englewood Cliffs, NJ. 1982. 183p. $12.95. (ISBN 0-13-039099-2)

Basic for the Apple II: Programming and Applications. Larry J. Goldstein and Martin Goldstein. Robert J. Brady Co., Bowie, MD. 1982. 250p. $14.95. (ISBN 0-89303-189-5)

Programming Your APPLE II Computer. Paul Bryan. Tab Books, Blue Ridge Summit, PA. 1982. 288p. $9.95. (ISBN 0-8306-1394-3)

ATARI

Atari Games and Recreations. Herb Kohl, et al. Reston Pub. Co., Reston, VA. 1982. 338p. $14.95. (ISBN 0-8359-0240-0)

Some Common BASIC Programs: Atari Ed. Lon Poole, Mary Borchers and Steven Cook. Osborne/McGraw-Hill, Berkeley, CA. 1981. 200p. $14.99. (ISBN 0-931988-53-5)

Your Atari Computer: A Guide to Atari 400/800 Personal Computers. Lon Poole, et al. Osborne/McGraw-Hill, Berkeley, CA. 1982. 458p. $16.95. (ISBN 0-931988-65-9)

COMMODORE

PET BASIC. D. J. David. Dilithium Press, Beaverton, OR. 1982. 150p. $7.95. (ISBN 0-918398-47-9)
Specific introduction to BASIC as it is used on the PET. Includes the use of PET graphics.

PET /CBM BASIC. Richard Haskell. Prentice-Hall, Englewood Cliffs, NJ. 1982. 154p. $12.95. (ISBN 0-13-661751-4)

PET Personal Computer Guide. (3d ed.) James and Ellen Strasma. Osborne/McGraw-Hill, Berkeley, CA. 1982.

Some Common BASIC Programs: PET/CBM Ed. Lon Poole, Mary Borchers and Carroll Donahue. Osborne/McGraw-Hill, Berkeley, CA. 1980. 200p. $4.99. (ISBN 0-931988-40-3).

<u>IBM PERSONAL COMPUTER</u>

IBM's Personal Computer. Chris DeVoney and Richard Summe. Que Corp., Indianapolis, IN. 1982. 303p. $14.95. (ISBN 0-88022-100-3)

IBM's Personal Computer: An Introduction to Programming Applications. Larry J. Goldstein and Martin Goldstein. Robert J. Brady Co., Bowie, MD. 1982. 302p. $14.95. (ISBN 0-89303-111-9)

<u>TRS-80</u>

Exploring Computing with the TRS-80 (and Common Sense). Richard V. Andree. Prentice-Hall, Englewood Cliffs, NJ. 1982. 230p. $18.95. (ISBN 0-13-296137-2)

Guide to Programming in Level II BASIC. Bruce Presley. Van Nostrand Reinhold, NY. 1982. unpaged. $12.95. (ISBN 0-942-25892-5)

BASIC APPLICATIONS

30 Computer Programs for the Homeowner in BASIC. David Chase. TAB Books, Blue Ridge Summit, PA. 1982.

Basic Computer Programs for the Home. Charles D. Sternberg. Hayden Book Co., Rochelle Park, NJ. 1980. 336p. $10.95 (ISBN 0-8104-5154-9)

BASIC With Business Applications. (2d ed.) Richard W. Lott. Wiley, NY. 1982. 306p. $16.95. (ISBN 0-471-08560-X)

Calculating with BASIC for Mathematics, Finance, Statistics, Mechanical Engineering and Electronics. Raymond Guido. Plenum Press, NY. 1979. 79p. $8.95. (ISBN 0-306-80144-2)

Simple BASIC Programs for Business Applications. J. R. F. Alonso. Prentice-Hall, Englewood Cliffs, NJ. 1981. 297p. $12.95. (ISBN 0-13-809889-1)

ADVANCED BASIC

GENERAL

Fifty BASIC Exercises. J. P. Lamoitier. Sybex, Berkeley, CA. 1981. 250p. $12.95. (ISBN 0-89588-056-3)

TRS-80

BASIC Faster and Better and Other Mysteries. Lewis Rosenfelder. IJG Inc., Upland, CA. 288p. 1981. $29.95. (ISBN 0-936200-03-0) Advanced techniques, some assembly language methods.

The Custom TRS-80 and Other Mysteries. Dennis B. Kitsz. IJG Inc., Upland, CA. 1982. 300p. (ISBN 0-936200-02-2)
Hardware and software modifications for special purposes.

Fast BASIC: Beyond TRS-80 BASIC. George Gratzer with Thomas G. Gratzer. Wiley, NY. 1982. 273p. $14.95. (ISBN 0-471-09849-3)
Disks or casettes available for programs in this book.

Microsoft BASIC Decoded and Other Mysteries. James Farvour. IJG Inc., Upland, CA. 1981. 312p. $29.95. (ISBN 0-936200-01-4)
Level II BASIC for the TRS-80 analyzed and explained in great detail.

Techniques of BASIC. John P. Grillo and J. D. Robertson. William C. Brown Co., Dubuque, IA. 1981. 256p. $18.95. (ISBN 0-697-09951-2)

ZX81 (TIMEX 1000)

Making the Most of Your ZX-81. Tim Hartnell. Reston Pub. Co., Reston, VA. 1981. 102p. $10.95. (ISBN 0-8359-04188-4)

The Sinclair ZX81: Programming for Real Applications. Randle Hurley. Dilithium Press, Beaverton, OR. 1982. 176p. $11.95. (ISBN 0-88056-090-8)

OTHER LANGUAGES

FORTH

Starting FORTH. Leo Brodic. Prentice-Hall, Englewood Cliffs, NJ. 1981. 348p. $15.95. (ISBN 0-13-842922-7)

FORTRAN

Microsoft FORTRAN. Paul M. Chirilan. Dilithium Press, Beaverton, OR. 1981. 325p. $15.95. (ISBN 0-918398-46-0)

LOGO

Apple LOGO. Harlod Abelson. BYTE Books, Peterborough, NH. 1982. 224p. $14.95. (ISBN 0-07-000425-0)

PASCAL

A BASIC Programmer's Guide to Pascal. Mark J. Borgerson. Wiley, NY. 1982. 118p. $9.95. (ISBN 0-471-09293-2)

Fundamentals of Microcomputer Programming, Including Pascal. Daniel R. McGlynn. Wiley, NY. 1982. 368p. $14.95. (ISBN 0-471-08769-6)

Elementary Pascal. Henry Ledgard and Andrew Singer. Random House, NY. 1982. 266p. $12.95. (ISBN 0-394-708800-8)
Identical to Elementary BASIC except that the language illustrated is Pascal.

Pascal Primer. David Fox and Mitchell Waite. Sams, Indianapolis, IN. 1981. 206p. $16.95.

Pascal Programming for the Apple. Theodore G. Lewis. Reston Pub. Co., Reston, VA. 1981. 234p. $12.95 (ISBN 0-8359-05454-4)

ASSEMBLY LANGUAGE PROGRAMMING

APPLE

APPLE Machine Language. Don Inman and Kurt Inman. Reston Pub. Co., Reston, VA. 1981. 246p. $12.95. (ISBN 0-8359-0230-7)

APPLE II Programming Exercises. Leo J. Scanlon. Wiley, NY. 1982. 192p. $9.95. (ISBN 0-471-86598-2)

Beneath the APPLE DOS. Don Worth and Pieter Lechner. Quality Software, Resada, CA. 1981. 166p. $19.95.

ATARI

The Atari Assembler. Don Inman and Kurt Inman. Reston Pub. Co., Reston, VA. 270p. $12.95. (ISBN 0-8359-0236-6)

TRS-80

TRS-80 Assembly Language. Hubert S. Howe. Prentice-Hall. Englewood Cliffs, NJ. 1981. 186p. $9.95. (ISBN 0-13-931121-1)

TRS-80 Assembly Language Subroutines. William Barden Jr. Prentice-Hall, Englewood Cliffs, NJ. 1982. 232p. $18.95. (ISBN 0-13-931188-3)

<u>ZX-81 (TIMEX 1000)</u>

Mastering Machine Code on Your ZX-81. Tom Baker. Reston Pub. Co., Reston, VA. 1981. 180p. $12.95. (ISBN 0-8359-4261-9)

The ZX-81 Pocket Book. Trevor Toms. Reston Pub. Co., Reston, VA. 1981. 128p. $10.95. (ISBN 0-8359-9524-0)

<u>SYSTEMS DESIGN</u>

The Elements of Programming Style. (2d ed.) Brian W. Kernighan and P. J. Plauger. McGraw-Hill, NY. 1978. 168p. $10.95. (ISBN 0-07-034207-5)

Etudes for Programmers. Charles Wetherhill. Prentice- Hall, Englewood Cliffs, NJ. 1978. $13.95. (ISBN 0-13-291807)

The Little Book of Basic Style: How to Write a Program You Can Read. John M. Nevison. Addison-Wesley, Reading, MA. 1978. 151p. $5.95 (ISBN 0-201-05247-4)
Nearly as classic as the Strunk and White book on writing after which it is patterned. Best design guide for beginners.

Software Debugging for Microcomputers. Robert C. Bruce. Reston Pub. Co., Reston, VA. 1980. 351p. $10.95. (ISBN 0-8359-7020-5)
One of the few books focussing almost exclusively on good design, error detection and testing of BASIC programs.

Software Design for Microcomputers. Carol Anne Ogdin. Prentice-Hall, Englewood Cliffs, NJ. 1978. 196p. $8.95. (ISBN 0-13-821801-3)
Technical design volume, intended for specialists developing assembly language control routines.

FOR USERS

OPERATIONS AND MAINTENANCE

CP/M Primer. Stephen M. Murtha and Mitchell Waite. Sams, Indianapolis, IN. 1980. 92p. $11.95. (ISBN 0-672-21791-0)

DON'T (Or How to Care for Your Computer). Rodnay Zaks. Sybex, Berkeley, CA. 1982. 264p. $11.95. (ISBN 0-89588-065-2)
Good introductory guide to the proper care and maintenance of a small computer. Warns of dangerous procedures, outlines recommended ones.

Microcomputer Data Communications Systems. Frank J. Derfler. Prentice-Hall, Englewood Cliffs, NJ. 1982. 129p. $12.95. (ISBN 0-13-580712-3)
Covers telecommunication hardware and software for APPLE, TRS-80, Atari, Heath, Commodore, and CP/M systems.

Microcomputer Operating Systems. Mark Dahmke. BYTE Publications, Peterborough, NH. 1982. 227p. $15.95. (ISBN 0-07-015071-0)
Detailed discussion of the CP/M, MP/M and UNIX operating systems for micros.

Osborne CP/M User Guide. (2d ed.) Thom Hogan. Osborne/ McGraw-Hill, Berkeley, CA. 1982. 280p. $15.95. (ISBN 0-931988-44-6)
This is an excellent general guide to the CP/M operating system. Despite the wording of the title it does not refer strictly to the Osborne I microcomputer.

PROGRAM SUPPORT

Apple II Word Processing. Carol Poling. QUE Corp., Indianapolis, IN. 1981. 250p. $19.95. (ISBN 0-88022-005-8)
Describes printers, add-in boards, CRTs and several WP programs for this machine.

Introduction to Word Processing. Hal Glatzer. Sybex, Berkeley, CA. 1981. 210p. $12.95. (ISBN 0-89588-076-8)

Introduction to Wordstar. Arthur Naiman. Sybex, Berkeley, CA. 1982. 202p. $11.95. (ISBN 0-89588-077-6)

An Introduction to Visicalc Matrixing. Harry Anbarlian. McGraw-Hill, NY. 1982. 252p. $22.95. (ISBN 0-07-001605-4)

The Power of: Supercalc. Robert E. Williams and Bruce J. Taylor. Management Information Source, Portland, OR. 1982. $9.95. (ISBN 0-13-687301-4)

The Power of: Visicalc. Robert E. Williams and Bruce J. Taylor. Management Information Source, Portland, OR. 1981. 88p. $9.95.

The Power of: Visicalc, Vol II. Robert E. Williams and Brian L. King. Management Information Source, Portland, OR. 1982. 97p. $9.95

Wordstar Made Easy. Walter A. Ettlin. Osborne/McGraw-Hill, Berkeley, CA. 1981. 125p. $7.95. (ISBN 0-931988-69-1)

The Visicalc Book: Apple Edition. Donald H. Beil. Reston Pub. Co., Reston, VA. 1982. 301p. $21.95 (ISBN 0-8359-8398-6) hardback. $14.95 (ISBN 0-8359-8397-8) paper. Excellent text for Visicalc. Index, bibliography and exercises. Probably the best teaching guide to date.

The Visicalc Book: Atari Edition Donald H. Beil. Reston Pub. Co., Reston, VA. 1982. 298p. $19.95 (ISBN 0-8359-8394-3) hardback. $14.95 (ISBN 0-8359-8393-5) paper. As for the Apple edition, above.

REFERENCE AND PROFESSIONAL MATERIALS

Despite the large number of publications, there are only a modest number of reference works and guides in this field as yet. There are a few printed indexes, one of which is on-line in the DIALOG system, and a small number of dictionaries and similar reference books. There are two journals which are directly concerned with microcomputer usage in libraries and only one book. The many books and periodicals concerned with the use of micros in school and other educational environments are, however, not included in this guide.

INDEXES, DICTIONARIES AND ENCYCLOPEDIAS

Basic BASIC-English Dictionary. Larry Noonan. Dilithium Press, Beaverton, OR. 1981. 150p. $10.95. (ISBN 0-918398-54-1)
Alphabetical guide to all common BASIC statements, allowing translation from one version of the language to another.

The BASIC Handbook: An Encyclopedia of the BASIC Computer Language. (2d ed.) David L. Lien. Compusoft Pub. Co., San Diego, CA. 1981. 480pp. $19.95. (ISBN 0-932760-05-8)
Compendium of all BASIC instructions, commands and functions. Cross-references to variations in many different BASIC dialects.

Computer Dictionary for Everyone. (new ed.) Donald D. Spencer. Scribners, NY. 1981. 192p. $5.95. (ISBN 0-684-16496-0) Microcomputer-oriented revision of an earlier (1977) edition. Well-reviewed.

Computer Programs in BASIC. Paul Friedman. Prentice- Hall, Englewood Cliffs, NJ. 1980. 270p. $10.95. (ISBN 0-13-165217-6) Annotated citations to several hundred BASIC programs which have appeared in microcomputer journals between 1976 and 1979. Arranged by function of the program. Indicates version of BASIC, special features, etc.

Computerists Handy Data Book and Dictionary. Clayton L. Hallmark. Tab Books, Blue Ridge Summit, PA. 1979. 96p. $4.95. (ISBN 0-8306-1069-3)
Combined dictionary and tables, formulas, conversion factors, etc. for micro users.

Illustrated Dictionary of Microcomputer Terminology. Michael Hordesk. Tab Books, Blue Ridge Summit, PA. 1978. 322p. $8.95. (ISBN 0-8306-1088-X)

The Index. W. H. Wallace. Missouri Indexing Inc., Saint Ann, MO. 1981. 486p. $14.95. Cross-referenced index to 44 magazines, by general topic and specific machines. Most journals covered from their first issues to mid-summer 1981.

MicroComputer Index. 2464 El Camino Real, Suite 247, Santa Clara, CA 95051. Quarterly. $30/yr.
Quarterly subject guide to 32 microcomputer journals. Available on DIALOG.

Micro... Publications in Review. PO Box 489, Arlington Heights, IL 60006. Quarterly. $56/yr. (ISSN 0278-6931)
"Current Contents" with journal contents pages reproduced. Subject index.

PROFESSIONAL PUBLICATIONS

1983 Classroom Computer News Directory of Educational Computing Resources. Intentional Educations, Inc. 341 Mt. Auburn St., Watertown, MA 02172. Annual. 199p. $14.95. (ISBN 0-9607970-0-9)
Comprehensive guide to programs, suppliers, interest groups, educational organizations on both the national and local level. Good for any collection but especially for schools.

ACCESS: Microcomputing in Libraries. PO Box 764, Oakridge, OR 97463. Quarterly. $11/yr. (ISSN 0277-9784)
Articles, comment and reviews relating to using micros in libraries.

The LMG Report on Data and Word Processing for Librarians. PO Box 251, New Westminster, B. C., CANADA V3L 4Y6. 5 issues per year. $45(Canadian)/Yr.
Contains lengthy and detailed hardware and software reviews on matters of interest to librarians.

Micro Software Report: Library Edition. Jeanne M. Nolan. Nolan Information Management Services. Torrance, CA. 1982. 92p. $49.95.

Selection guide to over 200 micro programs of interest to libraries. Covers "standard" programs (word processing, spread-sheets) in addition to specific library applications — serials control, catalog card preparation, etc. Includes prices, vendor addresses.

Microcomputers and Libraries: A Guide to Technology, Products and Applications. Mark E. Rorvig. Knowledge Industries Publications Inc., White Plains, NY. 1981. 133p. $27.50. (ISBN 0-914236-67-9) Hardware, programming, systems installation covered. Good overall picture, though there are small factual errors.

Small Computers In Libraries. Univ. of Arizona, Graduate Library School, Tucson, AZ 85721. Monthly. $20/yr. (ISSN 0275-6722) Newsletter with reviews, news, tutorials, product and program announcements for librarians.

PUBLISHERS' ADDRESSES

Only the smaller publishers have been included in this list. The addresses of the major ones can be found in standard reference sources.

Design Enterprises of San Francisco, PO Box 14695, San Francisco, CA 94111

Dilithium Press, 11000 S. W. 11th St. Suite E, Beaverton, OR 97005

BYTE Publications, 70 Main St. Peterborough, NH 03458

Robert J. Brady Co., Bowie, MD 20715

Compusoft Publishing Co., PO Box 19669, San Diego, CA 92119

Hayden Book Co., 50 Essex St., Rochelle Park, NJ 07662

IJG Inc., 1260 W. Foothill Blvd. Upland, CA 91786

Management Information Source, 1626 N. Vancouver Ave., Portland, OR 97227

Nolan Information Management Services, 21203-A Hawthorne Blvd., Suite 5323, Torrance, CA 90509

Prelude Press, PO Box 69773, Los Angeles, CA 90069

Que Corp., 6515 E. 82nd St., Suite 110, Indianapolis, IN 46250

Quality Software, Resada, CA

Reston Pub. Co., 11480 Sunset Hills Rd., Reston, VA 22090

Robotics Press, 11000 S. W. 11th St., Beaverton, OR 97005

Sams, 4300 W. 62nd St., Indianapolis, IN 46268

Sybex, 2344 Sixth St., Berkeley, CA 94710

Tab Books, Monterey Ave., Blue Ridge Summit, PA 17214

TITLE INDEXES

PERIODICALS

BOOKS

AUTHOR INDEX
(Principal authors only)